# Overthinking

*Stop Overthinking. How to Create Productive Habits, Overcome Procrastination, Eliminate Negative Thoughts, and Develop a Winning Mentality*

By Thomas J. Feelings

# Table of Contents

# Introduction

I would like to congratulate you all first for purchasing this eBook copy of *Overthinking.* I am really very glad to see that you all have shown immense interest in learning about your own psychology and how to deal with various situations. Thinking too much is very common, and it can be found in the majority of the people around you. But, thinking too much about something is not going to help you in anyways when you fail to do anything about the same.

When you keep on analyzing, commenting, and repeating the same kind of thoughts all time, in place of just acting in actual, you are actually overthinking. This might hamper your future decisions, along with endeavors. It will be consuming all your energy along with time and will also be preventing you from acting in the correct way. It is more or less like revolving around the same thing again and again without changing the path which is required for reaching new points in life.

What you are most likely to experience in such a situation is anxiety, worry, and also lack of peace. We will be discussing the various methods with which you can overcome all the effects of overthinking.

There are various other eBooks available in the market on Overthinking. Thank you for choosing this eBook. Every effort has been made to make this book as much interesting as possible. Enjoy!

# Chapter 1: What Is Overthinking And What Are The Causes?

There are various situations in our lives when we keep on thinking about a certain thing all day long. You might think that it is completely normal when you keep on having thoughts about something, such as any situation, behavior, or even thinking about a performance that you will have to do after a few days. But, in actual, it is not. When you are thinking too much about something, you are actually overthinking.

Many people think that when you overthink, you are most likely suffering from overthinking disorder. But, in actuality, there is nothing like an overthinking disorder. There are various types of disorders that come along with anxiety when an individual engages himself/herself in rumination or overthinking, but that is not a disorder. When you cannot stop obsessing and worry over things, it can actually interfere with your life quality. You might be wondering that what actually is overthinking. Some of the psychological diagnoses that have been done in which an individual cannot actually stop their brain from overthinking are actually the signs of trauma, PTSD, panic disorder, separation anxiety disorder, agoraphobia, social anxiety disorder, or it could be the signs of some other form of illness.

When it comes to the topic of overthinking, you might even think of it as a symptom. For instance, an individual who suffers from panic disorder might also ruminate and keep on thinking when he/she is going to experience an attack of panic again. Such individuals are most likely to obsess over anything which could actually trigger the attack. They are not only suffering from anxiety now, but they are having now meta-anxiety as well, which is nothing but getting anxiety about becoming anxious again. Overthinking is very common. You are not required to have an anxiety disorder for engaging yourself in continuous rumination. You can say it is a part of the condition of human beings. All human beings overthink at certain points in their life. You might become very conscious about what you said or did to someone close to you, or you might also become worried about some performance at work or at any function. These are the examples when are most likely to get engaged with overthinking.

Some other examples of overthinking are:

- Worrying about how to measure up to the other individuals at work.

- Obsessing about what you should have done or said.

- Thinking about the worst scenarios.

- Obsessive kind of thoughts.

- Engaging yourself in 'what-if' situations.

Overthinking is actually pervasive in nature. But, it also comes along with required help for such conditions. There are many people around us who worry and obsess about such things that are out of their hands or control in reality. The most common form of treatment for this type of condition is CBT or Cognitive Behavior Therapy. CBT helps the sufferers to challenge their irrational or negative thinking, which ultimately helps in changing their thoughts into taking positive and productive shape. Let's learn about overthinking detail first.

## Overthinking

Most of you are familiar with the famous term 'anxiety disorder.' But, in most of the cases, people tend to overlook one certain symptom of anxiety disorder, which is overthinking. The primary definition of overthinking is to obsess or ruminate about something. Many people, while coming across this definition, might think of themselves as being overthinkers. Who actually does not think twice about something in their daily lives? Human beings have the nature of wondering about making the perfect choice from very small things like choosing the easiest route for the commute to choosing the correct restaurant for a dinner night or thinking about the safety and security of your family. It is very much normal. It is really a common thing to worry and also to overthink up to a certain extent.

But, overthinking does come with certain harmful effects that can impact on your emotional as well as mental health. When overthinking pertains to anxiety disorder, it is most likely to have excessive, overwhelming thoughts about anything which leads to stress, anxiety, fear, or even dread. It is not only about thinking excessively about something, but it is also actually having an obsession with something so much that it will be ultimately affecting the functioning of your life. When you start wondering or worrying about your life, friends, family or something else and if you do not have the issue of overthinking, whatever you are thinking about will be worrying you only for some time, and then after a certain point of time, you will be going on with your normal day. You worry at times but are not ruminating continuously. You are not finding that the worry is actually interfering with your everyday life. This is normal.

With overthinking as the ultimate result of anxiety disorder, the concerned person can always think about, and even they might not be obsessing on the same kind of thing every time, they actually remain concerned regarding something all the time. If you think that you are suffering from overthinking due to anxiety disorder, you might find that you must have experienced any of these situations:

- Having difficulty in going along or contributing to any conversation as you are most likely to go over the potential form of statements or responses or the opportunity to actually speak up has been lost.

- Continuously measuring your very own self with others and trying to figure out how you measure to them.

- Reliving all your past form of failures and mistakes all over again from time to time, and you cannot move away from your past.

- Focusing on the scenarios of worst-case.

- Reliving any past experience of trauma.

- Unable to slow down the pace of racing thoughts, emotions, and worries.

It is very unlikely to find out that two people are experiencing overthinking in the exact same way. Those who experience overthinking will find out that the ultimate quality of their life is being compromised because of the inability to control all of their negative thoughts along with emotions. It might make it difficult for you to move out and mix with other people or socialize, enjoy your hobbies, try to be productive at your work as your mind is most likely to spend a considerable portion of time along with your energy in thinking about particular thought lines. In severe cases, it might also become very tough to control your mind along with your emotions, and this might turn out to be very damaging for your own mental health.

It might turn out to be very difficult for you to make new friends or even to keep up with your already existing friends as you are most likely to struggle in communicating if anything goes wrong or might turn out to be communicating more than required. It can also be very tough for you to speak up as you are overly concerned about how you will be doing it right or what will be happening next. An individual who suffers from overthinking might even find it very difficult to continue with a general form of conversation or to interact normally in a casual environment.

The truth behind this is, overthinking can actually affect almost everything and anything in your life. It can affect the whole way in which you love to work with others, impact your very own social life, and will also be taking a toll on your very own personal life. In simple words, it can begin to wear away all your relationships with the people all around you.

## Causes of overthinking

If you are suffering from overthinking, you must have come thought about the question, what is the reason behind it? Why does it sound like an illness? Such questions are most likely to keep on coming. However, in most of the cases, the causes are overthinking are definite in nature. The most common causes are:

- **Caring:** You are most likely to suffer from overthinking if you care about certain people in your life. In such cases, you are most likely think of doing things that will be loved by your close ones, and at the same time, you are most likely to think that what they would think if anything goes wrong or something else takes place.

- **Lack of confidence:** You must have come across the saying that confidence is the key to success. It is something that can drive you to the top. When you lack it, you start overthinking. It is mostly because you cannot trust yourself and start doubting yourself after doing something. What this results in is overthinking along with under-performing what you do the best. Overthinking triggered by a lack of confidence might turn out to be deadly for your mental health as you will find it difficult to properly do anything or even decide to do anything just because of the fear that you will not be able to do the things right.

- **Thinking yourself of being at fault:** When you start thinking of yourself of being the center of everything and also think you are the one who is at fault, you are most likely to experience overthinking. In such situations, you will always be finding yourself at fault and start to think awkward situations that won't happen ever. It will also be stopping you from taking part in things that you love, and you are most likely to find it difficult to socialize with people around you.

- **Past trauma or incidents:** Overthinking can also crop up due to any past incident which you cannot actually forget or erase from your mind. It can be an incident of extreme sorrow or an event of great humiliation where you were ashamed of doing something wrong.

Human beings overthink as we are desperate living beings who are always hunting for some answers. Human beings love certainty and also love to be in control. Not to be worried as it is also a part of the survival tactic of humans. Overthinking is nothing but 90% of fear of 10% of unwanted thoughts. Human beings cannot predict the future, and that is why we are most likely to overthink certain situations like what will happen if we do this or what will be the reaction of others? Will I be able to pull off the performance properly? This ultimately results in ruining the actual scenario, and you are most likely to end up underperforming.

The intuition of human beings gives out half of the ability to do that. Human beings come along with a very powerful voice inside, which actually helps in saving us in various situations, but at times, it might also dysfunction just because of overthinking. So, it is necessary to cope up with overthinking to get the best from our lives.

Overthinking is coupled, along with fear. Fear acts like the seed of a treacherous form of a tree. Human beings are not born along with fear; it adapts with the imparted life lessons along with traumas and life experiences. Human beings have very little or almost no control over what was done or taught to us in our childhood. The majority of the people who are suffering from overthinking are actually living with the branches of fear inside them from which they are developing their extra thoughts. Various things happen with us in our relationships, childhood, jobs, and friendships, and the worst part of those experiences are most likely to latch with the rest of our lives.

The past experiences and thoughts surface like the settled form of poison, which oozes through the human brain in the moments of overthinking. You are responsible for creating such patterns of thought. You keep on thinking about what happened with you in the past, and the ugly part of such experiences is most likely to trigger overthinking. You need to remember that the more you think, the more amount of fear you will be inviting in your life. Overthinking can have adverse effects on human lives, and it can alter the normal styles of living. If you think that you are suffering from overthinking, follow the tips in the following chapters for getting away from it.

# Chapter 2: How To Overcome Overthinking?

What is the thing which is actually holding back most of the people today from the lives which they wish to or want to live? The answer is both destructive and common in nature, and the thing is nothing but overthinking. People today tend to overthink even the minor problems until and unless it actually turns out to be big and much scarier than its initial phase. People who suffer from overthinking have the tendency to overthink even the positive subjects until they change their actual form, and it does not look positive anymore. Overanalyzing minor things do deconstruct the actual scenario, and thus, the happiness which comes along with it disappears without you having any idea about it. It might happen that you are in actual searching out for happiness, but when you overdo something, it is very natural to go out of hand.

Thinking about various things in your life is a great thing in life. But, when you get lost in the thoughts, that is when your thinking takes the shape of a disorder, and you are most likely to self-sabotage all the good things that try to happen in your life. When you start to overthink, all your judgments tend to become cloudy, and your level of stress is most likely to get elevated. You will be spending the majority of your life with the negative aspects. And, with time, it might turn out to be really difficult to cope up with. If you think you are also getting trapped within this very territory, it is high time that you take a step backward and start thinking about yourself.

## Tips to overcome overthinking

Here are some of the tips which can help you in getting back to your past life and start behaving and thinking like the good old days.

- **Being aware is the best option:** Right before you can start to address or even cope up with the habits of overthinking, you are required to learn to be actually aware when it is taking place. Right at any moment of time, when you find yourself overthinking or doubting, feeling anxious or stressed, all that you need to do is to step back and see the situation along with the way in which you are dealing with it. You will be finding the very seed of improvement and awareness, which can actually change you.

- **Do not think about the wrongs things always:** In the majority of the cases, overthinking takes place because of one single emotion, which is fear. When you start to only focus on the negative aspects which might happen, you are most likely to get paralyzed. The very next time when you find yourself getting in that direction, just STOP. You need to visualize each and everything in a situation and try to find out those things which can go right and try to keep up with all those thoughts.

- **Try to distract yourself into happiness:** Sometimes, all that you need is just a simple distraction to happiness. Finding alternatives to happy, healthy, and positive aspects can help. You can opt for various things such as dancing, meditation, exercise, knitting, painting, and music, which can help in distancing your very self from all the negative issues and will also cater to shutting down your traits of overanalysis.

- **Putting everything in perspective:** It is very easy to transform things into a bigger size, along with making them look more negative than they actually are. The next time when you find yourself in making a huge mountain out of a mole sized hill, just ask yourself how it is going to affect your life and matter in the next five years. Just this kind of simple question by changing up the frame of time can help you in lowering down your pace of overthinking.

- **Do not look out for perfection always:** This thing is really a major one. For each and every human being who is just waiting for perfection, the best thing that can be done is to just stop waiting for perfection. It is really a great thing to be ambitious, but when you start to look out for perfection all the time, that is the moment when everything turns out to be unrealistic, debilitating and also impractical. The very moment when you start to think about making anything perfect, the best thing that can be done by you is to remind your brain that it is not a smart thing to wait for perfection all the time and progressing rather than holding on will be better for your life.

- **Changing the view of fear:** Whether you are scared as you have already failed in the past or you are just frightened in overgeneralizing or trying some new failures, just remember that as you have failed once in the past does not mean that will be result or outcome every time you try. Each and every opportunity that you get in life needs to be treated as a new start.

- **Putting on a timer for yourself:** You can start to set up a boundary for yourself. Set up a timer for 5 minutes and devote that time to yourself in worrying, thinking, and analyzing anything you want. After the times goes off, sit down with a paper and pen and give 10 minutes in writing all those things which are actually worrying you, making you anxious or making you stressed out. After the timer of 10 minutes goes off, just throw away that paper and indulge yourself in some fun activity.

- **You cannot predict your future:** Human beings do not come with the superpower of predicting the future. All that we have for our life is now, this very moment. If you just waste the current moment in thinking and worrying about your future, you are only robbing the time from yourself. It is not at all productive in spending all your time thinking about the future. Try to spend all the time that you have on all those things which actually make you happy.

- **Learn to accept the best that you can give:** The most common feeling which is related to overthinking is the very feeling that you are not perfect or good enough, you are not hardworking like others, or you are not at all dedicated. Once you are done with giving your best shot, just accept that effort as your best. You need to learn that success might depend on some part on various things that cannot be controlled by you. You have given your all that you could have and stay happy with that.

- **Being grateful:** It is not possible to have a grateful thought and a regretful though both at the same time. So, why not spend the time with some positivity? Try to make a list every day of the things of which you are grateful.

- **Set shorter limits of time:** When you are not having a time limit when you need to make an important decision, that is the time when you start to turn your mind around across various things that are much away from the actual angle. So, all that you need to do is to learn to make your decisions in a better way. Try to always spring into action by simply setting up fixed deadlines for your life. Do not just depend on whether the decision is big or small. For all your small-sized decisions like if you need to respond to any email or do all the dishes or just work out, give yourself a time frame of only 30 seconds or even less for making such decisions. For the bigger kind of decisions that could have taken some weeks or days for you to decide if you are an overthinker, give yourself a time frame of thirty minutes or to a maximum end of the day.

- **Avoid setting up the day for overthinking and stress:** It is not possible readily to avoid a stressful or overwhelming day. But, what you can do is to minimize the total number of such things from happening in a week or month by setting up a good start to the day and by not setting up for a day of unnecessary suffering, stress, and overthinking.

1. Getting a good start: The way in which you are going to start your day will often be responsible for setting the tone of your entire day. When you start off your day in a stressful manner, you are most likely to spend the rest of the day in a stressful way. What you can do to give a kick start to your day? Try to read something positive while at the breakfast table or start jogging. It will be helping you in staying positive all day long.

2. **Focus on single tasks along with regular brakes:** When you delve into one single task at a time, it will help in developing a sharp focus all throughout the day. Also, do not forget to take short breaks in between as it helps in keeping the mind on the right track and also helps in improving your focus.

- **Getting good night sleep:** This might be regarded as one of the neglected forms of factors which can help in keeping up with a positive mindset and can prevent you from getting lost in the negative thoughts. When you do not get enough sleep at night, your mind gets more vulnerable to pessimism and worrying. It will also be preventing you from thinking with a clear mind. If you are having troubles in getting good sleep, try these tips:

1. Many of you have the habit of sleeping in warm beds and also in a warm set up. But, in actual, you will get good sleep when you keep everything cool. It helps the mind to relax and can also calm your sense, which will ultimately result in good night sleep.

2. Use earplugs if you get awaken by even a simple noise. Using earplugs will keep you away from all sorts of noises.

3. The most important thing is not to force yourself to sleep. If you do not feel sleepy, stay away from the

bed. Try to delve into reading some nice books or listen to soft music. This will help you in feeling sleepy faster, and you will also end up getting more amount of sleep.

- **Disrupt and then reconnect:** If you ever feel that your mind is overthinking too much, just disrupt all your thoughts at that moment and ask yourself to STOP. Reconnect with the current moment by spending 2-3 minutes in focusing on the things which are taking place around you. Try to feel everything around you; see them, sense them, and hear them.

- **Try to spend more time with people who do not overthink like you:** When you are trying really hard to get away from overthinking, your social environment actually plays a big role. This not only includes groups or people who are close to you but also what you listen to, read, and even watch. For example, forums, books, blogs, music, and movies in your life. Spend time with those people who actually impart a positive light on you and encourage you to think in a more positive way.

- **Realizing that you cannot control everything in life:** When you try to think about things 100 times can be the way when you actually tend to control everything in your life. You need to remember that everything in life cannot be controlled. The person whom you admire has also failed in their life and has learned from their mistakes, and that is what allowed them to become who they are now today. Don't just think about winning always. Make mistakes as that is what will be training you in getting better with what you want to. You will not be able to visualize any future scenarios. Mistakes are made by the winners. One day you will fail, and the next day, you will be able to master the same thing from all your mistakes, and that is what will help you in getting better day by day.

# Chapter 3: The Power of Habits

Whether it is for the good or worse, the habits that we carry on with us actually shapes us along with our lives. The daily lives that we spend are nothing but a complete series of all our habits which are played together throughout the day. Better forms of life habits come with the potential of increasing our well being and also come with the capability of performing effectively. The nature of human beings is all alike, and it is our habits that separate us from others. So, let all your bad habits in life can actually hold you back. You need to start building up new habits for making your life productive, happier, and also fulfilling.

When it comes to overthinking, it is a human psychological problem which also involves various habits. In fact, overthinking is built up of several habits that can actually hold you back in your life. Here are some of the habits which can actually help you in breaking all the chains and move forward in your life.

## Enthusiasm is very common whereas commitment is hard to find

It has found from various surveys that around 55% of the people who try to change their way of living actually fail in bringing about the transformation last not beyond a period of more than 6 months and an average individual tries to make the similar resolution of changing their lives almost 10 times without any signs of success.

When you actually know what you need to do is not actually an issue, committing to the same is the actual problem. Most human beings lack the proper form of structure, which can actually support their changes in behaviors that are required by the goals of their lives. The structures come with three broad pillars: commitment, patience, and consistency. All that you need to do is to put yourself in the conditions which will actually encourage you finding out a new way. Try to make new engagements, which will turn out to be incompatible with all the past ones. Try to envelop all the resolutions with all the aid which are known to you. Trying to make meaningful as well as effective changes which will be long-lasting as well in your life actually depends on the ability of the individual to form and then execute all the new activities for achieving new goals in life in a consistent way which will turn out to be a habit with time.

Overthinking comes with the negative thread of holding back to the past. Unless and until you let those threads cut-off, you will not be able to recover from the pain of overthinking. Always remember, overthinking can actually ruin your life, and it has the capability of throwing away all those ties in your life, which actually matters to you and thus leaving you all alone with your unnecessary thoughts. If you sense that you are suffering from overthinking, take your time and try to figure out what are the things which are holding you back, try to list them out. When you find out the list, try to kick those thoughts out of your mind and try to set up new goals. You will also require to make this thing consistent in nature in order to succeed in the real way.

## Spending the early hours of the day in finishing the high-value tasks

Do not try to start with your daily activities until and unless you have no idea about your day plan, which you want to accomplish. Don't just merely start off your day if you haven't planned it properly. Every day, try to get one of the most important and crucial things done in the first hour only. The easiest way of triggering yourself in finishing off with the toughest job is to get the work done during the first hour. When you start utilizing your mornings for all your high-value works, your mind will find it a lot more easy in cooing with the rest of the day as you are already done with the toughest job. When you try to keep the high-value works for the last hours of the day, your mind will naturally feel tired with all the work it has done throughout the day, and you will end up in overthinking the situation which will ultimately ruin your life and will also not allow you to get your work done.

You will need to lean forward to avoid all the busy jobs, which actually adds up no value to your work, life goals, or vision. Activities that are of low-value nature, which includes jobs like responding to your social media notifications, reacting to a friend's email, etc. will actually keep you busy and will ultimately prevent you from getting done with the real type of work. You will need to learn to make time for all those works which matter in your life. If you fail in paying the required attention to the things which have all your attention, it will end up taking a lot more of your attention than it actually deserves. It has been found that when a normal human being gets interrupted with unnecessary things, it takes up to an average of 23 minutes in getting back the concentration to the actual work.

## Practice single-tasking along with a purpose

In this age of continuous digital form of interruptions, no one needs to think a lot about why they are having problems in ignoring the various forms of distractions. If you really need to focus on any form of task, try to limit the time frame which you need to spend on that particular task. Start by adding dates along with the due times for your to-do list. You will need to push yourself in delivering the jobs within a specific time and then move forward.

When you mix up more than one job at a time, your mind is very prone to get distracted. When you get distracted, you are most likely to start overthinking and ruminating about all those jobs which are left to complete. So, try to do single-tasking at a time, along with no form of tolerance for all the distractions around you. You can start by focusing on one single job for a period of 30 minutes and then take a break of 5 minutes, and this will allow your mind to refresh itself and thus bring back your concentration again when you start doing that job again.

## Commitment for lifelong learning

The best way by which you can gain knowledge in your life is through self-education. It does not really matter if you are sitting in your classroom or in a coffee shop. As long as you are actually interested in the job which you are doing, do not stop. Try to make the most out of that time and try to get the best education that can be offered to you by yourself. Human beings who take out time along with initiative in pursuing knowledge all on their own are the ones who actually earn the real form of education. Most of the successful people in this world are nothing but a product of constant self-education.

Overthinking comes with a wide array of questions that your mind always finds out the answers for. When you start learning about various things around you, you can get most of your questions answered in the perfect way. Your mind will feel relaxed, and you can get rid of overthinking. You are not at all required to give out a considerable amount of your time in a day for the purpose of learning. The time which you decide on your own for putting in for your very own education, try to stick to the same. The primary goal is to seek as many knowledge and ideas which is possible within a stipulated amount of time.

## Using lateral thinking for solving all your problems

Lateral thinking is the job of setting out in looking at one of your challenges from a totally different angle for finding the perfect resolutions which could otherwise also remain hidden. Einstein said, 'Insanity is performing the same task over and over again but also expecting some different kind of results every time.' A new kind of approach is all that you require for getting unstuck. Try to break away from the vertical way of thinking. Vertical thinking involves the step by step way of analyzing the facts which are based on conventions and comes with one form of the expected result. Lateral way of thinking actually provokes you and will jump from one to the other, will break all the rules, and will look out for the new set of possibilities and will give out various results at a time.

Overthinking generally comes with a vertical form of thinking in which you think about the problems from one definite angle and are mostly expected to get stuck in your thoughts as the result which you are expecting will be the same every time you think about the same. When you stick to a problem and think on and on from one single angle, you will never be getting a successful answer to it. That is when overthinking takes over our lives, and ultimately, the result that you are most likely to get is ZERO.

Practicing lateral thinking comes with the techniques of solving all your problems from various angles at a time, which you can normally expect. It will not work when you keep on doing more of a similar kind of thing. So, working hard might not provide you with the result that you need and will leave you with rethinking only about the only approach which you are taking. Lateral thinking requires you to have the mindset of breaking off all the rules which are not rules in actual; they are the ways in which all the things have been done during the older days.

## Spending only 5 minutes  a day and being mindful

At any point of the day, when you are very much aware that your very own mind is wandering around, you are actually halfway in reaching the point of successful practice of mindfulness. Mindfulness is nothing but paying proper attention to each and every thing that is taking place around you. According to various researches, it has been found that those people who practice this regularly actually had some excellent effects on their minds.

With the help of continuous mindfulness practice, the activity of the human brain gets redirected from the past, including the reactionary brain parts along with the limbic system and then to the newest rational section of the brain, which is the prefrontal cortex. Sometimes, achieving mind calmness is all that you need to do with starting off your day in the right way. Mindfulness is not required to be practiced in a period of 30 minutes, just like the sequence of meditation. All that you are required to do is to start living in the very present moment. Overthinking has a lot to do with your past.

In the majority of the cases, people tend to hold on to past incidents and keep on juggling the thoughts of the same in their minds throughout their life. When you just stop dwelling around your past days or even worrying about the future days, you are open to a wide source of information which you have lacked in actual. It includes the information which can actually keep you out from the spiral of downward nature and get poised for a rich life. When you practice mindfulness in the proper way, it will alter your mind's operating system. In less than just a few minutes, you can easily turn out to be less reactive in nature and get attuned to the current moment. Within the period which you decide for practicing mindfulness actually lies the very opportunity for yourself to actually improve your way of making decisions and also direct the very way in which you mix with all the people who are around you.

The best time when you can practice mindfulness is early morning, but you can also practice it any time of the day you feel like. It will be helping you in selecting all your responses and will help you in making calculated moves in place of just succumbing to all the reactionary forms of decisions each and every day.

## Start reading everyday

When you indulge yourself in reading, you actually put your mind and brain to work. Reading is similar to the mind as of exercise to the body. It will provide you with the freedom of roaming the wilderness of time, space, history, and will also offer you much deeper views of concepts, ideas, body, and emotions regarding knowledge. Reading can be compared with praying, thinking, talking with your close ones, express your ideas, listening to the ideas of others, listening to music, enjoying the view, or also walking on a new beach.

Your mind on books is actually in the active state, changing, growing, and also making new types of connections along with various forms of patterns that are completely based on the material type which you are reading. When you indulge yourself in reading, you are actually heightening up the connectivity of your brain. Human brains change and also develops in a fascinating way when you read. When you read, your brain is actually decoding a long series of symbols of abstract nature and also synthesizing all the results into various forms of complex ideas. It is really an amazing process.

Overthinking requires you to indulge your brain into something different so that your mind can break away from the definite boundary of your thoughts and reach new heights. The reading state of the human mind can also be compared with the collaborative approach of orchestra symphony in which different parts of the brain works together in harmony, just like the various instruments for maximizing the ability to decode the written form of text right in front of you. It can be stated that reading actually rearranged the actual organization of the human brain, which in turn helps in expanding the very ways in which human beings think and which also changed the intellectual form of evolution of the human species. Reading involves the functioning of various functions of the brain, such as processes involving auditory and visual senses, fluency, a phonemic form of awareness, comprehension, and various others.

The exact same regions of the brain neurology get stimulated at the time of reading, which is also the same when experiencing it. Reading much away from listening or watching to the media provides the brain with much more time to just stop, think, imagine and then process all the narrative, which is in front of you. When you practice reading every day, it can help in slowing down the late-life form of cognitive decline and also helps in keeping the health of your brain in a good state. In this world of today, in which information is the new form of currency, reading can be regarded as the very source for the continuous form of knowledge, learning, and also acquiring much more than the currency.

Reading involves diligence, patience, along with determination. Thus, it also helps to calm down all your senses. It is more or less like any skill which you need to practice constantly each and every day. Next time when you select any book from your shelf or download anything new from the internet, just stop and try to think what you are actually reading. The things that you read in actual plays a great role in impacting your brain, which is much more than you can actually realize.

## Exposing your inner self to various views of the world

You are required to be curious in the genuine way for the new languages, cultures, or how various things are being done by the other people. When you delve yourself in various cultures, you can easily have a positive form of effect on your very own ideas. Try to find out how the various forms of work are being done in the various markets. The primary goal is to step out of your own perception of life. You are required to be open to new discussions that will not at all share your view of the world.

Overthinking will try to captivate you within a definite boundary about which you are most likely to think about all the time. Try to find out new topics so that you can divert your mind from the regular path of your thoughts. Start by reading all the books on those topics which you generally like to ignore. It is a proven way of protecting and reinforcing all your beliefs, opinions, and perceptions. The one and only way by which you can get out of the very world of yours is simply by stepping outside the boundary of your perception and start to embrace all the new forms of knowledge.

Try to get fascinated and attracted by new things. Unless and until you get fascinated, you will not care about learning something new. You will be only going through all the motions. But how can you get fascinated by something new? It is very easy. When you do something with or for some other people can help you in motivating yourself for looking deep down into something new or which is unknown to you. Just allow your inner self to wander around.

## Taking a break for restoring the flow

Many a time all that you need is to just restore the flow. Just take a few steps back and ask yourself where are the present patterns leading you to and whether you are progressing in the same or not. In case you start feeling stuck in some different arena of your life, just break away from the norm. When was the very last time when you actually broke the flow of your life and thoughts? When you start to take breaks every now and then, you can easily concentrate in a better way. Just stop staying in one single spot for too long and move on. When you find yourself lost in your thoughts or when you simply overthink, you can take a short walk for 15 minutes. It will help in relaxing your brain and will also allow more oxygen to your brain and thus resulting in better thoughts along with results.

# Chapter 4: Practical Guide to Develop Productive Habits

One of the many hard things for most of the people today is to change their already existing habits of a personal kind. Whether it involves the implementation of some new and good form of habit or it is just breaking away from the old and bad ones, it might feel like an impossible task for switching all your routines, which you actually followed for several years. But, it is not actually impossible to create or drop the habits; all that it takes is just a bit of willpower along with lots of dedication. We are actually what we do repeatedly. And, so does excellence, which not just an act but a solid habit. In our regular lives, it might be tough to build up new habits as there will be various forms of distractions that will lead all of us off from the narrow and straight path of achievement and will bring us back to the old path.

Wouldn't it be great if everything that we do could be automated? Starting from the way in which you start off your day to how you function the whole day and ending with the way in which you put a full stop to your day. For alleviating all the troubles which human beings generally face while changing their habits or developing productive habits, there are certain tips and tricks which you can actually follow for succeeding in this venture of yours. Let's have a look at them.

# Intentional repetition of all the good habits at least for 30 times in a day

Human beings come with the characteristic of having any repetitive event for at least 30 times right before it turns out to be normal. For instance, an executive who keeps on speaking without any kind of variation in his voice is most likely to bore the audiences. If the executive really wants to get the posture and use up gestures for creating vocal variations, he/she needs to engage in that way in both formal and informal settings. The executive will be able to stick to that habit after he does the same for about 30 intentional forms of instances. When you want to develop something good, try to stick to that thing for at least 30 times a day, and you will find yourself in getting accustomed to the same.

## Understanding the payoffs of associated nature

Each and every human behavior is being governed by the payoffs. Human beings stay pleasant to others as they receive a payoff. Human beings are also rude to others as we receive payoffs. So, in case you are trying hard to adopt a new habit or drop any existing one, try to dig in deep and understand the associated form of payoffs along with the habits. You can then easily decide to either connect with the receiving payoff or cut off yourself from the same.

## Understanding your very own values

All our choices actually help in revealing all of your values along with our priorities. If you are trying to break off from a habit, all you need to do is to first understand what is actually important about the very habit of yours. Many a time, it will be comfort in which you might feel comfortable in keeping up with a particular habit. Try to replace the same with a priority, which is of much higher value for you.

## Improving your environment

The fastest way for building good habits is to start by constructing consciously your existing environment, which includes your office, home, group of friends, transportation, and many others. All that you can do is to change your daily routine. When you let all those things go off, which actually holds you back, you will naturally look out for the new options which are available for nourishing your mind and body. For example, if you are a person who loves to watch videos all the time, you can change that habit by removing all the major sources of video from your life and shift to listening to podcasts. When your life isn't able to find the regular things with which it became habituated to, you will easily adapt to the new things for filling up the gap in your life.

## Setting your intentions and scheduling all your habits on the calendar

Habits are most likely to develop by the repetition of the same kind of actions continuously. When you decide to cut off with a bad habit or start with a new one, you need to be intentional for achieving the results. For the purpose of stopping any bad form of habit, you need to set up the intention of changing it and also replacing the same with a new and good one. When you stick on to a regimented form of plan, you can easily form productive habits by simply scheduling any task on the calendar, which will also be reminding you of what you are supposed to do.

## Setting up eventualities of if/then

The prime obstacle which comes in the way of forming or breaking any habit is the moment when you get tempted or when you slip up. So, it is always better to set up the possible form of scenarios from before only so that it becomes easier for you to take out the uncertainty out of your way. For instance, when you get tempted to eating a large piece of cake, just try to replace the scene by drinking a glass of water and then just count up to 10. When you are able to notice and break away from the impulse, there are high chances of you in reducing the breaking off of your word.

## Having a powerful form of 'why'

When you fail in committing to a powerful form of why you will be doing something, suppose any habit which you want to throw away or build, it will be nearly impossible for you to stick to it. If you by yourself can manifest a powerful form of why and also commit to the very reason why you need to change or make a new habit, the probability of ending a habit or gaining a new one turns out to be more.

## Making your very new habit the very first thing which you do every day

When looking forward to starting off a brand new habit for the first time in your life, the easiest way in which you can do so is to start off your day with the new habit every day. Your new habit, for example, exercising, praying, meditating, etc. needs to be the very first thing which you do every day as you get up. This will help in giving your brain the very importance of the new habit, and it can adapt to it in a faster way.

## Pairing or replacing

Pairing or replacing can be regarded as two of the most effective ways in which you can replace a habit or build a new one. For instance, if you need to jog more and you just love to listen to podcasts, make a rule that you can only listen to your favorite podcasts when you jog. You can try out many other alternatives for the already existing habits or try to pair them with something which you love the most. This helps in developing a determination to practice the new habit.

## Getting a partner who is accountable

When you try to adapt some productive habits all by yourself, you might not succeed all the time, or you might not be able to commit to that habit. You are most likely to get more motivated when you can find a person of supportive nature who can hold you accountable to all your goals. Try to explain and share your goals with that person. You can ask your partner to hold you accountable for your goal with the help of phone calls, email check-ins, a motivational form of conversations, and various other things. Motivation from a supporting person can help you in achieving your goals much faster than usual.

## Starting off small and building good habits slowly

You can start by building up a keystone habit of good nature. The keystone form of habits comes with a rippling effect on the lives of individuals who are trying to start something new. In case your goal is to get healthier, you can start by drinking a glass of water every day when you wake up in the morning. As you become successful for a period of two weeks, you can up the game by adding another glass of water to your already existing habit of consuming one glass of water. The primary goal of this is to slowly reinforce your mind that keeping up with good habits is better for you and is easy as well.

**Keeping up with the practice even when you fail**

The productive form of habits arises right from the brain patterns which are grooved in and also takes up something for interrupting and creating the new neural form of pathways. It involves plenty of repetition, along with continuity. The main goal is to keep on practicing and also giving yourself the chance to fail. And, all that you are required to do is to just keep on practicing. The main difference between ending up a bad form of habit or starting off with a new good habit might be a gap of one practice only. So, don't just stop if you fail.

## Try to give all your focus on the 3 Ps

When you are determined to change a habit of yours, just try to focus on the 3 Ps, which are practice, patience, and perseverance. Patience is needed as it takes up some time to build new habits. Practice is needed as it is needed to keep up the activity in a recurring order in order to shift your habit from being mindful of being habitual. Perseverance is required, as you are most likely to face lots of moments of frustration along with setbacks in your way. Try to keep up with all of these, and you can easily hold up the new habit.

## Creating a list of wins

Wins are most likely to create momentum. For the very purpose of getting inspired to create productive habits or to break away from a bad habit, you are needed to focus on the daily number of wins. When you win for a day, your one win can help in changing your entire life. Each and every individual is required to know their list of wins, and also they would like to achieve the win. When you can develop the clarity regarding what you actually want to achieve, it will help in increasing all the odds of achieving the same.

## Starting off from the present

You can start by assessing if you are ready or not to bring about the new habit. In case you are still thinking about the change, and you are also finding yourself in a defending position from the current form of patterns along with your systems of beliefs, you are not actually ready now. For the goal of creating a long-lasting change in your behavior, you are required to be committed first for changing yourself, and then only you can prepare your mind to take up the required actions for transforming the changes into a regular habit. Just start off from where you are at the moment and follow the path.

# Swishing

You can visualize yourself in performing the bad form of habit. The very next moment, try to visualize your very own self where you are actually trying to push away the bad habit and also performing the alternative. You can end the sequence with the very picture of yourself where you are in a state of high positivity. You can run this exercise several times in a day, and you will notice that your tendency to practicing bad habits is going away slowly with time. Picturizing yourself gives you an image of your future, which will guide your brain in stopping from performing the bad habit for your very own good.

## Doing it for yourself

Stop worrying about all such things which you think should have as your habits. Try to tool all your habits right towards your very goal along with all the things which actually motivate you. Empty kind of resolutions is not at all enough in sticking the productive habits with your life. You need to realize that it is for your very own good. You are the one who is responsible for breaking yourself down and also building yourself up.

## Knowing all the benefits

Try to get yourself accustomed to all the benefits which you can achieve from changing a habit of yours. When you are able to figure out the benefits, you can easily notice a change in your energy levels along with your enthusiasm for adapting to the change.

## Write them down

Many people tend to achieve what they want in life by simply writing their goal on a piece of paper and keeping the writing in front of them. It actually helps your mind to adapt to your enthusiasm for getting the change and also helps in increasing your motivation.

## Processing the plan

The step which most people skip while fantasizing about having a productive form of habit is that they do not answer clearly why they actually want this change in their lives. It might look like a very small detail, but in reality, it actually plays a deep part in keeping up with your motivation over the course of time. Only visualizing what you want to achieve is not going to help. Try to plan out the image along with the end results properly.

## Running the change as a new form of experiment

It might happen that you want to bring about a change in your habits, but you are not sure about the end results. You can overcome this by adapting the new change as an experiment, which you can carry on for a week or two. You can easily assess the results, which will be in the form of changes in your life and try to compare the same with your past. Is it better than before, or it is of no use in your life? When you run a new habit as an experiment, you can get a clear idea about the results and can also gain the required motivation by getting sure about the end results in the long run.

## Using 'but.'

The best way in which you can bring about a new change in your life is by thinking about your current condition with 'but.' For instance, you can use but for interrupting all your negative thoughts like, 'I am not at all good at doing this, but if I keep on working, I might succeed one day.' This actually works like magic as it helps in contrasting your present situation with the future where you can easily see the end result and get motivated in going with the change.

The habits that you adopt for yourself are for your own good. If you think of any of your habits as ruining your life, do not think twice and just start working on from now only. If you start now, you can easily enjoy the majority of your life under the lights of positivity with no shadows of negativity around you.

# Chapter 5: How To Overcome Procrastination Step By Step

Assume that is Monday afternoon, and the time is passing by. You are finishing up all your works furiously for submitting the same before 5'o clock, which is your deadline. At the same time, you are also cursing yourself for the reason for not starting the work on time. But how did this happen? What is the thing which went wrong? What made you lose your focus from work? Well, the reason is the hours of the day which you spent in scrolling down your social media, re-reading all your mails, taking longer coffee breaks, and also the time which you spend on those tasks which could have been easily done after a few days. All of these happen because of procrastination.

Procrastination can be regarded as a trap in your way to success. It is nothing but the practice of doing the less urgent types of works with more preference in place of the ones on which you should actually work. It results in the delay of the important tasks and thus often resulting in failure.

## Is procrastination and laziness the same thing?

Procrastination is often compared with being lazy, but in actual they are two different things. Procrastination is an active kind of process in which you can choose to do some other kind of work in place of the one which you know should be done. Unlike procrastination, laziness comes along with inactivity, apathy, and also unwillingness for acting in the desired way. Procrastination generally involves ignoring those tasks which are unpleasant but are also important in nature in favor of those tasks, which is much more easier or enjoyable.

When you give in easily to the impulses of procrastination, it might provide you with some serious form of consequences. For instance, even the slightest incidents of procrastination can make you feel ashamed or even guilty. It can also result in a reduced degree of productivity and can also cause you to easily miss out all your achieving goals. When you keep on procrastinating for a long time, you are most likely to become disillusioned and also demotivated with all your important works, which can also eventually result in depression and even joblessness when it goes out of hand.

## How can you cope up with procrastination?

As with most of your habits, it is actually possible for us to deal with procrastination. You can follow the mentioned steps below for dealing with and for preventing procrastination.

- **Recognizing that you are actually procrastinating:** You might have the tendency of putting off any task as you need to re-prioritize the workload that you have. If you are knowingly delaying a task which is important in nature for an actual good kind of reason, you are not at all procrastinating then. But, in case you start to put the tasks off in an indefinite manner or just simply switch your focus every now and then as all that you want is to avoid a particular thing, then you are most likely to procrastinate. You might also find yourself procrastinating in case you:

    1. Try to fill up your whole day with tasks that are of less or no priority in actual.
    2. Leaving any item on your list for a very long time even when you know that it is important for you.

3. Reading all your emails many times without even taking any form of decision on what you are required to do with all of them.

4. Starting with a task of high priority and then taking a long break for no reason at all.

5. Filling up your routine with the tasks of other people instead of the ones which are important for you to get them done on time.

6. Waiting for the perfect mood or for the perfect time always for tackling any tough task.

- **Working on the reason why you are probably procrastinating:** You are required to understand the very reasons why you are actually procrastinating right before you start with the processes of tackling it. For example, are you having the tendency to avoid some particular sort of tasks as you are finding them unpleasant or boring in nature? If that is the case, you need to take your steps out of the same very quickly so that it becomes possible for you to easily focus on each and every aspect of the tasks so that you can find them more enjoyable. Poor form of organization can also result in procrastination. People who are of organized nature can easily overcome the traits of procrastination as they are of the habit of using a prioritized form of to-do-lists and can also create an effective form of schedules. Such tools can help in organizing all the tasks by deadline and priority.

It might happen that even if you are organized in nature, you might get overwhelmed by any task. In case you have any doubt on your very own ability and you are also worried about the thought of failing, you are required to put off that particular task and find out for comfort in some other kind of work which you know you have the capability of completing on time and perfectly. There are various people who have a fear of success, exactly like the fear of failure. Such people have the tendency to think that success will make them filled up with more requests by others for taking some more work. But, surprisingly, the people who are actually perfectionists by nature are also procrastinators. Such people would often avoid doing any kind of task which they feel incapable of doing and would rather on the tasks which they could pull off perfectly.

Another cause related to procrastination is poor form of decision making. In case you are not even able to decide what you should be doing, you are most likely to decide to take up the wrong action and finish the thing in the wrong way. For many people, procrastination might even turn out to be more than just a mere bad habit. It might also be a sign of an underlying issue of health. For instance, anxiety, depression, OCD, and ADHD are also linked along with procrastination.

It has also been found from various studies that it might also be the cause of any serious form of illness and stress. So, in case you are also suffering from this debilitating or chronic form of procrastination, you can blame these many reasons, and it is high time for you to start with the process of coping up with the same.

- **Adopting various strategies of anti-procrastination:** Procrastination is often referred to as a habit, which is a kind of behavior of deeply ingrained patterns. In simple words, you will not be able to break its spell overnight. You can stop your habits from being the habits by avoiding practicing them and so you are required to take up any of the strategies mentioned below for succeeding from the grip of procrastination.

1. You can start by forgiving yourself for procrastinating in the earlier days. It has been found that self-forgiveness comes with the power of making you feel much more positive than usual regarding yourself, and it can also help in reducing the chances of procrastination in the upcoming days.

2. You can prevent procrastination by committing to the tasks. You are required to focus on doing the tasks and not just avoiding them indefinitely. You can do this by simply writing down all the jobs that you are required to finish and also specify a time frame for the same. This will be helping you in tackling your works in a proactive way.

3. You can also ask someone else to continuously check on you. It is true that peer pressure actually works. This is the prime principle on which the self-help groups rely on. You can also opt for self-monitoring in case you have no one to check up on you.

4. You need to act up as you go. Tackling all the tasks as soon as you receive them instead of just piling them up can help a lot.

5. You can rephrase the dialog of your inner-self. Various phrases such as 'have to' and 'need to,' for instance, helps in implying that you are left with no other choice in doing what you are supposed to do. This might even result in making you feel disempowered and can also result in cases of self-sabotage. But, when you use phrases such as 'I choose to,' it helps in implying that you are owning a project, and it can also make you feel having control of the entire workload that you have.

6. Minimizing all your distractions is of prime importance. Try to turn off your social media along with your email and also avoid sitting in a place that is close to the television for your work.

7. Try to do all those tasks which you do not like in the first hour of the day. This will help in making you feel more concentrated on doing the tasks which you love.

**Tip:** There is also an alternative form of approach which embraces the subtle art of delaying. According to various researches, an active form of procrastination which is delaying all your tasks deliberately so that you can give your focus in doing the urgent jobs can help in making you feel much more challenged along with motivated for getting all the things done on time. This approach works specifically if you are the kind of person who actually thrives under extreme pressure.

In case you are procrastinating as you are finding a particular task very unpleasant or boring, you are required to actually focus on the long form of the game. It has been found from various studies that people who are of impulsive nature are most likely to procrastinate as all that they are focused on are the short-term gains. You are required to fight against this by recognizing the long-term gains or benefits after you complete the entire task. Another effective way of making your work feel more enjoyable is by identifying all the unpleasant form of consequences for avoiding the same. For example, imagine situations that what is going to happen in case you do not complete the task? How is the situation going to affect you personally, your team, or even organizational form of goals?

In case you procrastinate only because you are disorganized by nature, follow these tips, which can turn you into an organized person.

1. Try to create a to-do list. This helps in preventing forgetting all your tasks, which are unpleasant in nature.

2. You can try to prioritize some of the specific tasks in your to-do list. It helps in the identification of all those tasks which you should actually focus on along with the ones which you can actually ignore.

3. Try to use the method of scheduling and planning. When you are having a big-sized project or various projects at one time, and you are not aware of the

point from where you should start, you can try out planning and scheduling which also helps in using up all your time in the most effective way and also helps in relieving your stress.

4. Try to tackle all the tough jobs at your preferred peak time. Do you work your best in the afternoon or early in the morning? Try to find out your most effective time so that you can finish all the hard tasks within that period of time.

5. Set up goals that are bounded by time. When you set up particular deadlines for completing all your tasks, you can easily be on track for achieving all your goals, and thus, you will be left with no time for procrastination.

6. You can try out various applications for the management of your tasks. If you are unable to plan out your schedule, such tools can help you in planning properly.

If you are very much prone to delaying all the projects as you find them overwhelming, you can try to break them in small and manageable forms of chunks. You can easily organize your schedule when you have small chunks of tasks to be completed, and you will also find it a lot easier to start with them.

- **Taking a break:** It is important for you to give your mind a break of 10-15 minutes whenever your work timer gets off. Try to listen to music, read books, or take a short walk in that period of time. It will help your mind to concentrate on the hard task again and will also make you feel more motivated than before. When you work on constantly without taking any kind of break, your brain is very likely to get overworked and ultimately results in getting blocked with all your works. Try to give your mind the space it needs for breathing, and after you return to work from a short break, you can easily find out the difference in your confidence and concentration, and thus, you will be able to finish off with your work quickly and also in the perfect way.

- **Getting rid of catastrophizing:** One of the very reasons why people procrastinate is because they tend to make a large deal out of a very small thing or simply catastrophize. You are most likely to catastrophize when you feel stressed with work or feel bored in completing the task. So, when you stop catastrophizing, you can easily get your work done like all the tasks which you love without any signs of procrastination.

- **Being realistic:** Fooling yourself by acting that a particular task won't take much time is not the ideal thing to do. Try being as much realistic as you can. Don't just provide yourself with up to the mark time. Try to bake in some extra time so that you can finish the work peacefully. When you hurry with any job, you are most likely to procrastinate as you might feel stressed or anxious about the work. Giving your job a little extra time will provide you with the peace of mind which you need to get your job done on time.

- **Rewarding yourself:** Who doesn't love rewards? Right? Try to set up rewards for your very self as you finish up your work on time. If you love being on social platforms, try to set the same as your reward, which you are not going to use unless and until you finish off with your work. It will also provide you with the motivation that you need.

# Chapter 6: Remove Negative Thoughts And Negative Influence

We, human beings, view the entire world via our mental makeup and attitude. If, in any case, this attitude of our mind turns out to be negative predominantly, it can actually impact everything in your life, which also includes your health, family, career, and various other aspects of your life. Along with that, negative thoughts come with a spiraling kind of effect, which attracts more amount of negative thinking. Negativity which wells up inside us or in our surroundings can quickly turn out to be very toxic in nature, and it can also hold us back from living the kind of life which we actually want. Luckily, you can slowly train your inner-self with time on how you are supposed to think by the implementation of very easy and simple techniques.

## Techniques for getting rid of negative thoughts

Let's have a look at some of the techniques.

- **Having regular time for negative thoughts:** It can be regarded as a paradoxical kind of strategy for gaining control over your negative form of thinking by committing around ten minutes every day for reviewing and ruminating all your negative thoughts over and over again. NTT or negative thought time needs to be for at least 10 minutes and also needs to be practiced every day. When you are having any sort of negative thought during the course of your day, try to jot it down and ask yourself that you will be reviewing the same during your NTT. With time, you will be able to gain complete control over your negative thinking, and it will also be stopping eventually.

- **Replacing all your negative thoughts:** You cannot overcome your negative form of thinking, but you can actually replace them. For most of the individuals, the patterns of negative thoughts are well-worn pathways of neural nature. It comes with four very simple and easy steps:

  1. Properly notice the time as you start the pattern.

  2. Acknowledge that it is the very pattern that you want to be changed.

  3. Articulate all the aspects which you want to be in a different form.

  4. Choose a different kind of behavior, the behavior which you feel actually serves your target or goal.

- **Being your own best friend:** Human beings are the meanest to themselves. Almost 90% of the self-talk is of a negative nature. You are required to follow three steps for overcoming this:

1. Release all that you have. Let the negative thoughts out for helping the process and not for dwelling with it.

2. Track it down. Properly identify when you are actually having negative thoughts. When you become aware of your negative patterns, it will be helping in reframing all your thoughts.

3. Reframe all of your negative thoughts. Once you have understood it clearly why you are so mean to yourself, try to think what your best friend will be telling you in such a moment. Then just tell your inner-self all those things which you actually need to listen to.

- **Writing in place of just thinking:** Try to write down why your negative thoughts are present. When you replace thinking with writing, it helps in purging out all your thoughts out, and when you are able to see all the words on a piece of paper or on a screen, it will become easier for you to make sense out of the same and then just move forward with it.

- **Making conscious efforts for finding out things to like, love and appreciate:** Instead of just fighting all your negative thoughts, you can reach out consciously for the thoughts which can make you feel a lot better. One of the powerful ways of doing this by speaking out loud, if possible, by you to what you like love and appreciate. Are you heading into a tough kind of thought? "I really love the taste of coffee today", "I really like the way of seating out here", "I would appreciate all the chances of processing all these ideas with my team". Such statements to yourself can help you in reaching out for the relief, and you can find it also very easily.

- **Asking yourself tough natured questions:** You can reflect all your answers on some tough kind of questions.

  1. What do I actually receive in life with these patterns of negative thinking?

  2. What am I getting as a reward for this?

  3. What am I losing in life for engaging myself in the negative nature of thoughts?

  4. What will I gain from positive thinking?

  5. What is the reason behind the patterns of negative thinking?

  6. What am I supposed to do now?

When you question yourself all of these, you can easily find the answer to your solution.

- **Establishing new kind of habits:** Rather than just thinking of the process in terms of overcoming all your negative thoughts, you can think of the same in terms of establishing some new kind of habits. You can achieve this by directing all your senses and attention to those subjects where there is no requirement of overcoming anything. These could include subjects which you already feel nice about, and thus you can think of the subject in a positive way. The subject could be your very own pet, your love for traveling, your liking for being on the beach, etc. You can always start with something which is very easy by nature.

- **Prevent yourself from watching the early morning news:** It has been found from various studies that even 3 minutes in the morning of negative news can easily increase your very chances of a negative kind of experience over the natural course of your day. It has also been found that the positive nature of mindset can easily improve your productivity and can also provide you with satisfaction along with reducing your rates of making errors. Mindset is your very own choice but might not be an easy thing always. Look out for eliminating all the negative form of influences from your life and also stop watching the morning bulletin or news.

- **Using affirmations:** As you wake up every day and open your eyes, try to feel the gratitude for a fresh new day. You can write down affirmations daily, such as: 'I love all the people whom I work with,' 'I try to make positive nature of contributions every day' or 'I am always open for inspiring thoughts.' In case any negative thought creeps in your mind, try to think of a success which you have achieved recently along with the feeling which you experienced at that moment. Positive thinking is a daily form of the task but is also worth all the results.

- **Developing the success routine:** You can do this by taking out some amount of time every morning as you wake up and then meditate. You are required to focus on the kind of person which you actually want to become in your life along with the great quality of life which you have been planning to live in the future. You are required to set up some new sort of goals for keeping up with the momentum of building up slowly in the direction of your dream. When you actually have the idea about what you want from life, and you are constantly trying to achieve the same, you will see that negativity will slowly fade away from your mind.

- **Channeling all the negative thoughts into something productive:** The patterns of negative thoughts can take over easily, but a great trick is to properly identify the pattern of your negative thinking along with a job that you are really excited about. Every time when you find out that you are focusing only on the negatives, try to refocus all your thoughts for a period of 10 minutes on your very new project which you are excited about. You can easily channel all your negative kind of thoughts into your new project.

- **Focusing only on gratitude:** Gratitude is often regarded by most of the people as being underrated, but in actual, it is very important for leading a happy life. Life isn't going to become easier, but you will become stronger day by day as you learn to reframe all your difficulties in your life by identifying all the little sort of things which is actually going around you. You can keep up with a good list and try to refer to the same daily. Try to focus on the things which you really want in your life and also try to be very specific when you identify your goals. A focused and positive kind of mind will easily attract what it actually wants over time.

- **Try out meditation:** It is not possible for anyone to escape from their negative thoughts unless and until you disrupt them physically. For getting all your negative thoughts out of your mind, you are required to get into your own body. You can do this by opting for breath work for a period of 10-15 minutes, or body movements such as yoga can help in disrupting all your negative thoughts. Yoga and meditation come with proven powers of positivity, and it can readily help in calming all your senses so that you can concentrate on positive kind of thinking.

- **Not paying attention to what others will say:** When you start concentrating on what other people will say about you if you do something or do not do something can readily impart negative thoughts in your mind. In such situations, you are most likely to zap all your personal form of power and fall in the trap of analysis paralysis. When you actually get stuck in all such thoughts, you will actually drag yourself much more away from reality. The truth is that people around you do not have that much time, energy or attention for thinking or talking about anything that you do. People around you have their own world where they have their pets, kids, jobs, families along with their very own worries and fears.

This sort of realization or rather a reminder can really help you in setting yourself free from all the constraints which you are most likely to build up in your mind and will also help you in taking the required steps for achieving what you actually want in your life. In case people say anything about you, try not to pay attention and enjoy your own way of living your life.

- **Questioning your thoughts:** The best thing that can be done on your part when negative thoughts tap on your shoulder and tries to grow in your mind is to just question the thought. Just ask yourself: 'Should I take these thoughts in a serious way?'. This will often lead you to answers where you are not required to pay any sort of attention to the negative sort of thoughts. When you are tired or hungry or get overworked, negativity can easily crop up in your mind. Try to focus all your inner answers on the positive aspects of your life. You might also come across answers from your inner-self when you find that just because you have made a small mistake, that does not mean that you will be getting the whole thing wrong. When you question your thoughts, you are actually performing a reality check.

- **Replacing negativity in the surroundings:** All the things which you allow into your mind each and every day will actually have a big effect on your life. Try to figure out the sources of negativity in your life. It might turn out to be any person, magazine, website, music, and various other things. Try to ask yourself what can be done by you for spending the least amount of time with the sources of negativity in your daily life. When you can successfully analyze the sources of negativity in your life, you will be able to distance them away from you. You will be able to see the results readily where you are most likely to find yourself as a completely changed person.

- **Stop creating mountains from the molehills:** For the very purpose of stopping a very small negative kind of thought from taking the shape of a huge monster in your very mind, try to comfort the same at the earliest as possible. Try to analyze the thoughts with questions like is it going to matter to you in the next 2 years of your life? When you find out that you have been actually creating a mountain from a molehill, you can easily get away from the negative thoughts which have been building up in your mind.

- **Talk it over:** When you start piling up all the negative thoughts in your mind without letting anyone know about the same, you are actually doing great harm to yourself. Try to let all your negative thoughts out by talking about the same with someone close to you. When you just vent the thoughts only for a few minutes, it can actually help in seeing the overall situation in new lights. If you cannot have a conversation about your negative thoughts with someone, try to have some positive kind of conversation, which can help in boosting up the positive side of your mind.

- **Not letting in the vague fears:** One of the most common types of mistake which most of the people make when it comes to the aspect of fear is that they become very scared of the same and try to run away from the very situation instead of just giving it a closer look and trying to fight it over. It is actually very natural when you feel this sort of impulse, but when the fears are actually vague in nature, they might turn out to be scarier than they really are. Try to examine the situation like: What is the worst that could happen in this situation? When you actually realize the result of the fear and figure out that the end result isn't that bad as you think, you can easily fight it over. You can also start to opt for listing and taking various actions of a few of the things in your life which could actually decrease the very likelihood of the worst scenarios from taking place. You can easily gain clarity about the very situation and can gain all the strength that you need for fighting over the fear.

Negativity and patterns of negative thoughts are destructive in nature. It can actually ruin your way of living or the goals which you want to achieve. If you find yourself in situations where negative thoughts are filling up your mind, take action immediately, and try to use the mentioned techniques for fighting it over.

# Chapter 7: Mindfulness and Positive Thinking

If you have dipped in the sector of positive psychology, you must have discovered the most popular topics of today, which is mindfulness. It is a broad part of human psychology, which has evolved in the last few years.

## What is mindfulness?

It is nothing but the act of maintaining all the moments of your very own feelings, thoughts, surrounding environment along with bodily sensations via the lens of nurturing and gentle nature. Each and every human being in this world is wired towards the aspects of negativity. You can easily get caught up in the cycle of rumination, along with worrying and imagining about each and every possible outcome of your future. This often leads to an increased amount of anxiety along with lots of stress.

But, when you keep all your thoughts moving in the direction of positiveness, it will not only make you feel good at that very moment, but it can also help in reducing your degree of sadness to a great extent. Moreover, it can also provide you with the one and only thing that all human beings require for keeping up with their lives: HOPE. The more you engage yourself in employing positive thinking and mindfulness in your life, the longer the efforts will be lasting.

## Meditation based on mindfulness

You must have come across the term 'mindfulness meditation.' If you think that what is the real difference between mindfulness and meditation based on mindfulness, then there really isn't any such major difference. Mindfulness is referred in the general attempts for incorporating more amount of mindfulness in the life of an individual whereas, meditation based on mindfulness is the kind of practice which is often seen as the most stereotypical form of meditation with you sitting with your legs crossed and eyes closed while engaging in the activity of basic meditation for a certain time period.

Typically, mindfulness meditation and mindfulness often refer to the same kind of concept in which you stay aware and open up your inner-self and also allow all your thoughts along with your feelings to take place without any kind of judgment. The only form of distinction which can be found in between the two is that the concept of mindfulness meditation comes with the connotation of turning out to be a kind of practice which is time-constrained in nature.

The most common question which is often found regarding mindfulness is that whether it is a trait or a state? This question is of utter importance for someone who actually dabbles in mindfulness. Whether if it is a strength or a trait, permanent or less changeable is often a debate.

## Need for mindfulness and positive thinking

Have you wondered ever about what it actually means to live at the present moment? It is true that all of us are available right now at the current moment. But, only 10% of us are actually right here. All of us are actually living within our minds and thoughts. Human beings exist in a state of day to daydream where you are not connected with the world in actual and nor with your own being. Instead of that, all of us are actually preoccupied with all our past memories, where we are busy churning our worries and thoughts about the future along with the reactions and the judgments of a few of the things which we actually see. You are missing out a majority of your life, which ultimately leaves you in feeling empty, shallow, and also unsettled in life. That is when you need to learn to be mindful and also to be at present. Let's have a look at some of the ways with which you can easily practice mindfulness in your regular life.

- **Eating mindfully:** When you actually gulp down your meal while being distracted by the computer, TV, or any form of constant conversation, you are actually missing out on the delicious taste and attractive smell of the food. You are also very less likely to actually feel nourished and satisfied after having a sumptuous meal as you literally missed out on the very fact of what you actually ate. In simple words, do not try to do 100 things at a time when you actually sit for having your meal. Try to focus on what you are eating as it has been proven that when you eat well, you feel good. Having a tasty meal can make you feel positive and happy when you actually have a meal in an enjoyable way.

- **Walking down the road mindfully:** There is a saying, 'walk in a way as if you are embracing the earth right with your feet.' In simple words, when you are out on the road all alone, try to pay attention to all the significant movements of your body along with the surroundings. Notice the moment as your feet connects with the ground and then leave it again. All that you need to do is to just observe what is actually going around you. When you try to take a walk all by yourself, you can actually connect with yourself in a better way than you can do at any other point of time.

Try to feel everything around you, the sounds, the sights, and the lives which are unfolding around you. If you are having negative thoughts or you are just ruminating, try going out for a short walk where you can connect your inner-self. You will be actually amazed to find out the results as you will be able to connect your heart with your mind like never before. You are needed to understand that you are your own best friend. So, try to connect with your inner friend for getting the most out of your life and enjoy the same to the fullest.

- **Observing the way in which you breathe:** One single breath in and out can actually work like meditation. The way in which you breathe occurs rhythmically and naturally. When you actually start to pay attention to the way in which you breathe, it can take you right out of your mind and will let you into your very own body. You will feel free momentarily from all the churning kinds of thoughts, fears, and worries in your mind, and you will also be able to recognize your true self by getting in touch with your inner soul and not with your regular kind of thoughts.

- **Connecting with all your senses:** The human senses- smell, taste, touch, sight, and sound- are actually the gateway of getting into the current moment. But, at times, when you remain lost in your thoughts, you will most likely not experience the things which your senses are sensing or picking up for your mind. You can achieve this by doing the simplest things, such as pausing for soaking up the fantastic aroma of your coffee, the salty kind of ocean wind, the diversity in your neighborhood, the beauty of flowers, and many others.

  You can also achieve mindfulness by noticing how the clothing is feeling against your torso or body, the clean and soft bed sheets on the skin every morning, the comfort that you get as you kiss your lover, and various other things. All that you need to do is to just put a little amount of love along with attention to the simplest tasks of your everyday life, and you will actually be amazed when you will realize the amount of peace and joy that you can actually bring up for yourself.

- **Taking a pause in between the actions:** You can try to pause at some of the simplest events in your life and just listen to the inner meaning. You can pause and feel your body weight in the chair right before you start working on your desk. The primary goal is to give mini pauses to your life in between various actions throughout your day, which can actually help you in reaching out to your inner-self, clear up your mind, and can also provide you with a fresh form of energy for all the new forms of tasks.

- **Listening wholeheartedly:** Most of us do not even listen to the people who are actually speaking to us just because we are engaged in the thought of what should be said next, judging all the things which are being said by various people or just getting lost in our world of daydreams. The very next time, when you find yourself in a meaningful conversation, try to make it your primary goal to actually listen to what is being said by the other person in conversation instead of just getting lost on your very own thoughts. This will also help in getting the actual message of the conversation as mindfulness is all about living in the present.

- **Getting lost in the flow of doing all the things which you love:** Each and every one of us has certain kinds of activities in our life which we love doing the most. Such activities actually help in connecting with our inner spirit and also help in bringing us alive. For you, it can be dancing, cooking, gardening, singing, painting, writing, swimming, cycling, etc. People often tend to love all those things which they often find losing themselves in. You can incorporate more flow in your activities in your daily routine, and you will find that your happiness will be reaching new heights.

- **Meditating daily:** Nothing can be better than meditation. When you start meditating regularly, you will come across various benefits like an increase in the levels of happiness, energy, inner peace, and inspiration. When you will find yourself getting lost in the thoughts or when you start overthinking, just take out some time and meditate. It is not needed to be more than just 10 minutes and only this amount of time in meditation can bring you wonders. It can provide your life with a positive impact. It will help you in strengthening up your muscles of mindfulness so that it becomes easier for you to be in the present moment all throughout your day.

- **Traveling or mixing up your entire routine:** There are various reasons why people feel so amazing when they are on holidays. When you visit a new place, you will become more mindful naturally and be in the present moment as there are various new sounds, sights, and smells in which you can soak up your inner-self. When you travel, your senses will take over your mind for a moment, and it will result in freeing up your mind right after that. Do not have any travel plans currently? No worries as you can mix up your entire routine for having the same kind of effect.

Try to take a different road, stop by a new café, try to visit a newly opened place or try to opt for something which you haven't done before ever in your life like cooking on your own without anyone's help, scuba diving, and various other activities. When you opt for new activities at regular intervals, you will find yourself to be more confident and creative than before, and your mind will open up to new opportunities and will be soaking in all that it can get.

- **Observing all your emotions and thoughts:** You are not actually your thoughts but the observer of all the thoughts. The very fact that you listen to all of them depicts that they are not actually you. You are someone separate and much higher than your thoughts. When you be aware of your thoughts and observe without judgmental eyes, you can be a part of the present. As you observe all your thoughts, you are required to resists all your temptations from getting carried away with them right down a narrow into your future or past. So, do not just get carried away with your thoughts.

# Benefits of practicing mindfulness

Mindfulness comes along with several benefits. The studies have found out that mindfulness can actually alter the human physiology of our minds and bodies in various ways so that they can be healed, strengthened, and protected. Let's have a look at some of the benefits of practicing mindfulness.

- **Lowers down stress:** Mindfulness helps in lowering down your physiological markers of deep stress and also helps in improving the ability of your brain to manage stress. It is done by improving the connectivity in those areas of your brain which is essential for executing all the controls.

- **Helps in restoring emotional balance:** Emotional incidents have the ability to knock you down from your balance. The damage which is done comes in great intensity, which can devastate your mental makeup. Mindfulness helps in improving your rate of recovery from any kind of emotional situation simply by keeping a check of the emotional part of the brain.

- **Helps in reducing anxiety:** It has been found from various studies can mindfulness can reduce the degree of anxiety in adults by up to a rate of 40%. It is done by increasing the amount of activity in that part of the brain, which processes all the emotional and cognitive forms of information along with that part of the brain, which controls the situations of worrying.

- **Helps in reducing physical pain:** It has been proved that mindfulness can easily reduce the physical form of pain without even activating the opioid system of the body. It also helps in reducing the potential for any kind of side effects of addictive nature. This is really beneficial for you if you experience physical pain very often and is particularly helpful for those who have actually built up a good system of tolerance for opiate-based drugs.

- **Helps in reducing depression:** It readily helps in dealing with depression as it helps in opening up your mind so that you can soak in all the positive energy from your surroundings and feel more motivated.

- **Helps in improving quality of sleep:** You can easily improve your sleep quality by practicing mindfulness regularly. It also helps in reducing fatigue along with insomnia.

- **Helps in improving concentration:** It helps in improving your executive form of attention and thus helps in improving your ability to concentrate on your task. Mindfulness also helps in ignoring all forms of distractions, which are most likely to act as the barriers in your way to success. Mindfulness comes with the same effects as undergoing therapy from a therapist. It helps in the building up of a positive form of energy, which ultimately helps in improving your senses.

# Chapter 8: How To Develop A Winning Mentality

You are required to have a grown mindset for making your life as great as you want. The prime key to achieving all the success that you want in your life is to adopt a winning mentality. Remember, the attitude that you carry forward with yourself plays a great role in determining your success rate. When you say that yes I will win in this, it is very easy to say so but really hard to do it in the right way. You have uttered such words surely for once in your life. No one in this world comes with the desire to lose naturally, but when you figure out that winning actually requires something more from you, you will be setting up a different kind of view for the same.

There are only a few in this world for whom winning has turned out to be a habit. Such people not only achieve what they want to, but they also do the same in a consistent way. The desire and will power of such people is so very strong that it is the only thing that actually helps in waking them up from sleep every morning. It is what makes them give it all they have while working for something which is really important for them. Such people are the ones whom we attribute by using the term gifted or really talented.

It is actually a very easy job to find out various reasons why other people come with the capability of winning and why we are failing constantly. Whenever we come across a winner, we are most likely to get caught in various vague words such as training, talent, and also circumstances as there are various reasons why you are not actually capable of winning the race. "He comes with a great build which provides him with the advantage," "They have the best facilities," "They have a great infrastructure," and various other statements are often made by us in various situations, and many a time, we also use them unconsciously. But, in actual, there is something more to the basic form of winning, something which actually accounts for the consistent form of success. The primary key for becoming a person who makes it a normal course to win every day is to adopt a winner's mentality, a mentality that all those people who achieve greatness maintain in a consistent manner.

Our body comes along with various limitations, but our mind does not. When you want to win something, you are needed to be mentally prepared for the same. You are required to have the mentality which will actually allow you to succeed in the game. This form of mentality is often referred to as the winning mentality. But, how can you define the concept of winning mentality? It is the mentality which you allow you to dig deep in the situation and do all which it takes in relation to putting the efforts, taking action, perseverance and also for inspiring others who are around you for the sole purpose of overcoming any kind of adversity which might come up in the way and will win at the end. It is like willing to do what others are afraid of doing consistently for gaining an advantage of competitive nature and also for mastering the craft for becoming the winner.

Such a form of mentality needs to come from your within, and it is not at all something which can be forced by anyone on you. Someone can tell you repeatedly for developing a winning mentality so that you can win the game, but if you do not have the urge by yourself to win, then no matter what others say, you will never be able to win. The winning mentality can be used in various aspects of life. Whether it is your professional field or any relationship of your life, it can help in all the aspects of life. In case you do not have this kind of mentality, it is possible for you to develop the same over time. So, do you have a winning mentality? Let's have a look at some of the traits which can easily depict if you have the winning mentality or not.

- **People with winning mentality pursue improvement relentlessly:** Those who are the winners know it very well that they won't be able to reach where they want to be staying in the same position, and all that they need is a constant improvement. For the purpose of winning, they know that they need to get better every day. It is not actually about any kind of competition; it is mainly about being your best, which you can be. The only thing which can limit the distance that you can go is only your mind. The winners have the habit of breaking the barriers relentlessly which prevents them from improving. They actually try to do what makes them feel uncomfortable in order to grow behind their zone of comfort. It is the only way in which you can turn out to be better than before and win ultimately.

- **They find a way for turning adversity into the fuel required for winning:** Adversity affects each and every human being around us. But, in place of just feeling guilty or sorry for themselves, instead of just putting all the blame on someone else or instead of just giving up, the winners know it very well that the only person who can turn them into winners and also change all the circumstances is only themselves. The winners do not have the habit of swimming in the deep pool of self-pity. They know it very well how to pick themselves up as they fail and how to continue with the journey. The winners choose not to actually shift all the blame on others and also accept all the responsibility for carrying the same on their own shoulders. Adversity, along with a bit of change in the opinion, can change into a great form of fuel, which will help in bringing about success.

- **They know that luck does not exist in reality:** Luck is nothing but the meeting of preparation with opportunity. When you actually believe in luck, you will start to believe that anything bad or good that you will be getting in your life is all up to chance. The true form of winners leaves nothing for the chance. Each and every one of us gets some kind of opportunity at a particular point in life, but when we are not actually prepared for it, we are most likely to waste it. Some individuals are always prepared and also win when they get their opportunities. The true form of winners actually tries to take it one step further; they try to create their very own opportunities with the help of sheer will power along with all the effort for making sure that they make the best out of what they have.

- **They do not love to give up:** The winners do not actually give up in any aspect of their life. When you actually give up, you are never going to win the battle. If you want to make your chances of winning consistently in nature, you are required to master the very art of successful failing. Winning can only be achieved after various attempts, which might also end up in failure and it is known to all the winners.

# The 3 C's related to winning mentality

Winning mentality comes along with various factors that can actually help you in winning the race. There are 3 C's which can help in attaining the winning mentality.

- **Competitiveness:** Winning is not actually everything, but your will of winning is actually what matters the most. In case you want to succeed in any arena of your life, you are required to want it in the true sense, have the capability of setting it as up an ambitious form of the goal and also have the grunt for working in order to reach your goal. When you turn out to have a mindset of competitive nature, you will find none of the obstacles as being too big for you, which you cannot overcome, no form of a challenge as really a challenge and no pain in the journey which cannot push you through. When you really want to win, you need to have that hunger in yourself which won't allow you to sleep peacefully. You need to have competitive thoughts, always running your mind. No matter what happens, just stick to it. Even if you fail numerous times, you will still be a winner to yourself as you know you have it all that you have.

- **Confidence:** The winners come with a silent form of confidence, which will occasionally provide them with enough self-belief which will actually be allowing them to perform at the highest possible level. Such a form of confidence can be attained from a disciplined form of practice, which helps in improving all the skills to a very high level along with quieting all those voices which doubt you and tell you that you can never win. When you are confident enough, you will never have the thought of getting lost. You will be persisting with the belief that the best is still to come which can only be tested at the end. Failing to have enough confidence in yourself, along with all your skills, can actually prevent you from reaching your goal. So, it is really important to level up your confidence right before you prepare to enter the game of reaching your goal. Lack of confidence will surely lead you to failure.

- **Composure:** Being composed of your own ability is important when you really want to win. Listening to the outside voices and feeling under-confident with your own abilities won't help. Try to be consistent with what you actually do and what your abilities are. It might happen that at times, your emotions will control your mind and prevent you from performing your best. At such moments, all that you are needed to do is to stay composed with yourself and focus only on the thing which you want to achieve.

# How to develop a winning attitude?

You can also develop a winning attitude by following certain techniques. Let's have a look at them.

- **Focusing on the passions:** Give yourself enough confidence only by focusing on those things which you love the most. It is much easy to develop a great form of attitude as you delve into doing something which you love. In case you are not at all sure about what you love the most, try to look into your daily habits. You will surely find out all those things which attract you the most and which you love to do.

- **Thinking positively:** Start with small things and try to feel positive with even the smallest things that you do. Repeat what you have been doing, and you will be able to develop a positive attitude for it. Think that have you been successful every time in your life? If yes, then why are you allowing the negative things to prevent you from giving your best as you that you will surely succeed? Try to figure out the very reason behind your thoughts. It will actually work and will help you in developing a positive attitude towards your efforts.

- **Slowing down the speed of emotions:** When you find yourself thinking in a negative way, try to take a deep breath. You are required to practice mindfulness regularly for calming all your senses. You can control all your racing thoughts when you practice mindfulness regularly, and you will find out that your automatic way of thinking will be coming under your control. It is most likely because our emotions stop us from sensing our surroundings. When you can actually learn to sense your surroundings, you will be able to develop a winning mentality as it helps our minds in gaining positive powers.

- **Setting up your goals high and monitoring the progress:** When you try to be realistic, it is not going to change anything. But, when you try to be unrealistic, it will actually help. Setting up goals that are much higher than your imagination can help you in setting up the will power which you need for achieving your limits. Try to enjoy the whole journey and also monitor your progress. Do not just focus on the end results as it will prevent you from achieving your limits. Try getting into the process and move out of the boundary of the outcome.

- **Commitment:** When you set up higher goals for yourself, it will be of no help unless and until you can commit to the same to the fullest. If you cannot commit to work towards the goal and achieve the same, you will lack the confidence that you need for your achievement. Commitment is something that can even help you in climbing up a mountain. You might also require to sacrifice various things in your life when you try to commit to achieving something. Remember, when you commit with your will, you will surely succeed.

- **Being true to yourself:** You are required to understand that winners actually quit. Those who are winners know exactly where to quit. You need to be true to yourself. In case you have winded up yourself in something which is not your passion in actual, try to be true to your inner-self and move away from it right away. You can look out for something else. It is your own life, and you have all the right to control it. Being fake to yourself will only be harming you. Try to be true and judge the situations in their real sense.

- **No excuses:** When you try to make excuses for not doing something or for not being able to do something, it is most likely to turn into a habit. You will be the prime victim of your very own vibrations. You are the one who is actually accountable for your actions and what happens to you. Learn to accept them and own them. When you try to ignore something by making vague excuses, you are actually instilling negativity in your own mind.

Each and every one of us is born with some potential of our own. We all come with something which will allow us to be the winners in our own life. All that you need to do is to just tap your inner potential and try to bring out your winning mentality.

# Chapter 9: The Power of Goals

Do you really know how to set up your life goals? How frequently you can actually achieve the large-sized objectives which are actually important for you? When you face problems in setting up your goals properly, you might even get tempted to stop all your tries. In such situations, people have the tendency to say things such as, 'Maybe this is what it is' or 'I should be contented with what I already have.' In case your goal is to lose some weight, how will you understand that your goal has been completed? When you have lost 1 kg or 20 kg? When you fail to have a clear form of a target, you can never hit the right mark. That is why it is so tough to learn about the various things for setting up your goals which are measurable, clear and also actionable.

## Why is it necessary to have goals?

An effective form of goal setting is the actual key to your success. Whether it is improving your intelligence, starting off with a new hobby, or restarting any relationship, when you set up goals, you can actually create the future right before it happens in actual. With goal setting, you can expand and grow in life which will be pushing you in the way which you might have never imagined before in your life. For the purpose of feeling fulfilled in the true sense, you are required to actually know what you are working on achieving something in your life. Progress in our lives is actually equal to happiness, and setting up goals besides it actually helps us in getting there. Most of the time, people think that they actually understand how to set up goals, but at the same time, they will not be achieving anything that they wanted. The very reason behind this is that the goals of such people were not inspiring or compelling nature.

Human beings are most likely to invest their energy along with time on something which actually excites them in real. So, all your goals need to reflect a similar level of excitement or momentum. You need to think of your goals as your dreams right with a definite deadline. All that you are required to do now is to just create up a blueprint for achievement.

**Two primary questions for compelling nature of goal planning**

- **Identifying the goals:** What is the thing which you want to achieve? What is the objective which you actually desire? Looking out for a promotion at your work? Or to opt for meditation daily? For selecting the achievable form of goals, you are required to have a clear form of outcome in your mind. A very magical thing happens when you opt for something or when you take generalized nature of desires and then start to define the desires in a more precise way with the help of a detailed form of goal setting.

- **Identifying the purpose:** Why are you looking out for achieving this goal? What is the result that you will receive after this? Will the promotion which you are looking up to give you freedom financially? For keeping your goals, you are required to ask the right form of questions, and then only you can seek real changes in life. When you know what you are actually moving towards, you will be able to find various ways in order to make the same thing happen. Always remember that the reasons always come in the first place, and they are the answers.

# Goals and its different types

For further identifying how you can create the best process of goal-planning, you are required to know the actual type of goal which you want to achieve or have. There are various types of goals that can easily divide into several categories, like health goals, fitness goals, relationship goals, career goals, etc.

- **Short-term goals:** This can be achieved typically within a period of less than one year, and it comes with things such as getting the promotion at work, lose 20 pounds, or building up a new home. While you look at the short-term goals in the process of goal planning, think of them as enabling your goals so that as you complete them, you can quickly move ahead for achieving the long-term goals.

- **Long-term goals:** These are much more extensive in nature and generally take much more time to achieve when compared with short-term goals. Examples of this sort of goal would include starting your very own business, opting for a cruise for your wedding anniversary, and many others.

- **Lifetime goals:** These goals are exactly of the type as they sound like. These are those goals that you actually want to achieve during the course of your life. It could be somewhat like retiring from your job at the age of 60 and then you want to participate in various mission trips with your partner. When it comes to the planning of goals for the lifetime goals, it would generally include the setting of capstone goals which are of similar nature as of enabling your goals.

## Creating and maintaining the momentum with S.M.A.R.T type of goals

There are actually very few principles that can guide you for setting effective goals that will help you be on track. The best of the lot is the SMART goal.

- **Specific:** The more detailed you become, the better it will be for you. How specific is it possible for you to be when your goal is losing weight? "I would like to lose 10 pounds" is actually a good form of a start but "I want to lose 10 pounds so that I can look good in my favorite dress" will make it much easier for you to visualize your goal and will also help in achieving it much faster. This actually helps in putting up a valid reason right behind your goal, which will ultimately allow you to preserve with all your plans, which you have developed at the time of setting your goals when things turn out to be challenging in nature.

- **Measurable:** When it comes to the time of the effective form of goal setting, keeping track of your progress might actually turn out to be critical. When you set up a clear form of parameters along with viewpoints, you can track down your progress, and you will also be able to know when you will achieve the goal. For instance, "turn out to better in money handling" is not a type of measurable form of a goal. It is actually unclear what the 'better' actually means here. You are required to have a solid form of metrics within your mind when you learn to set up your goals. Having the goal to have an idea about the present pattern of spending, paying off credit card bills, saving 20% of the income in each month- now you actually have some benchmarks which you can easily use for checking on your progress on your journey to success.

- **Achievable:** When you are not able to actually attain the goal which you have set at the time of planning your goal, it will only be frustrating you and will also be disheartening you. When you create your goals, try not to get too lofty, such as being the richest businessman overnight or be a world-renowned violin player within two days. Lofty dreams will actually make all of your goals to seem impossible in nature.

- **Realistic:** In an ideal setting of the world, you will have around 5 hours a day working on your tennis game. You are living in the real world. So, you are required to make sure that the setting of your goals actually matches reality. Is it possible for you realistically to become the best violin player when you have never touched an instrument in your life? The goal that you are setting needs to match with the current lifestyle of yours.

  But, this does not mean that it is not possible for you to dream big or opt for something which does not fall in your comfort zone. What it actually means that you need to be focused on the planning of goals on which you can work towards realistically. In case your goals need some time or any form of monetary commitment, you need to ensure that you have all the required means for doing so. Sometimes, it might be required to break down your dreams even further. It might not be possible for you to become the best violin player, but you can start taking up lessons for being part of a great concert.

- **Time frame:** When you have a clear idea about your timeline at the time of goal setting, it can help in creating a sense of real urgency. You will be able to move towards the thing which you want more faster than anything else. Try to set up a timeline for all your goals so that it becomes easier for you to check on yourself at the time of the journey. If you have short-term goals, try to create only those goals which can be achieved realistically within a time frame of one year. You need to concentrate on the short-term goals first for achieving the long-term ones in no time at all.

When you learn to set up goals that are SMART in nature helps in outing power right behind the goals and also makes sure that you can also measure all of your progress and also take up new actions.

**How to set the right goals?**

For the sole purpose of setting up the right form of goals, you need to follow certain steps:

- **Decide:** First, you are required to think about something which you want to work on or want to achieve. It does not actually what you choose, unless and until you want to do it. It might be something which you are really interested in or actually feel excited about. But, make sure that it is within your limits or reach. The goals that you decide for yourself needs to be for its very own sake and not actually for something which others are doing. It might be small or big in size. It has been found that when you divide your goals into small pieces, it actually helps in achieving them as when you set up goals, which stretch can be motivating in nature.

- **Write them down:** It has been proved that when you write down your goals instead of just thinking about them in your mind, there are high chances for you to stick to them. You need to write the benchmark for your goal, which will let you know when you have reached the destination and also the time when you will want to achieve the same. Write down how the goal actually connects with your life and describe them as much as you can. For instance, write down 'I want to plant some flowers in my garden in the month of May' instead of just writing 'I want to do gardening.' The more you write, the more it will be easier for you to achieve them. It will also allow you to plan up your goals and you can set up your schedules of life according to that.

- **Telling someone:** When you share your thoughts with someone, it is most likely to make you feel motivated and positive. In the same way, try to share your goals with someone in your life who actually matters to you. When you tell someone about your goals, it will help in increasing your chances of sticking to the same. It also helps in bringing about a positive change in your life, which you need for achieving certain goals in your life. It will also help you in feeling more determined, and you will find it easier.

- **Breaking down your goals:** This is a very important step for all the big type of goals. Try to aim on all the short-term or smaller goals, which will be necessary for achieving the bigger goals. The bigger sized goals might turn out to be a bit vague at times, such as, 'I want to be much more healthy.' When you break down such goals into smaller goals, it will be easier for you to achieve the same. So, a smaller sized goal like 'jogging daily' will help you in your venture. Write down all the smaller goals and also assign time for each by which you want to achieve them. The faster you reach your smaller goals, the faster you will be attaining the bigger goals. Having small sized goals actually makes the whole journey a bit easier and will also give you a sense of success on the way.

- **Planning the first step:** When you decide to walk 10,000 miles, you will need to put your first step. Even when your goal is not to achieve the 10,000 miles mark, just thinking about the very first step on your way can actually help in getting started with the journey. Even when you have no idea about where to start from, do not give any kind of excuse to yourself. You can do a research about the same before putting forward your first step. Always remember, when you try to give excuses to yourself, you are actually lying to yourself. Instead of just thinking about what to do, try to do something so that it can be regarded as your very first step. As you plan your first step, the rest of the journey will turn out to be easier for you.

- **Keep going:** When you start working on your goals, it might turn out to be really frustrating and difficult at times. So, all that you are needed to do is to preserve. When you find out that a step of yours is not actually working, try to look out for something else which can actually help you in moving forward a little bit. In case you find yourself struggling with something on your journey, ask for help from people who actually have some idea about your goals. In case you find yourself to be really stuck with something on the journey, try to take a break. After you are done with your break, try again. Trying only can help you in achieving what you want in life. Even if you fail, do not stop and just keep moving. When you fail, your chances of winning also increases a lot than before.

# Chapter 10: How To Sleep Peacefully?

Sleep is essential for each and every one of us. Human beings spend almost a third of their lives sleeping. It is actually important for us the same way in which breathing and eating are important for all of us. It is important for maintaining a proper form of physical as well as mental health. Sleeping comes with the power of recovering us from physical, along with a mental form of exertion. Health and sleep are both connected by the same string. Poor sleep can lead to the risk of having a poor form of health. When you have poor health, you will find it more difficult to sleep properly. Disturbances of sleep can be the first sign of distress. Common forms of mental health problems like depression and anxiety might often lead to sleeping problems.

Sleep is something from which we all can benefit in some way. For the majority of us, it might be as simple as just making a small form of change in the lifestyle or even adjustments in attitude which can help us in sleeping better. It has been found that around 1/3rd of the human population might actually suffer from the problem of insomnia along with various other sleep related problems. When you fail to have proper sleep, it is most likely to affect your energy, mood, levels of concentration, relationship, your ability to working at day time and various others.

But, it has also been found that even some basic techniques can be used for improving your sleep quality. You can consider four of the simplest things which can help you in healing from poor quality of sleep.

- **Health:** It is known to all that poor health is most likely to affect our sleeping pattern and vice versa. Mental health problems such as anxiety and depression might often be found going hand in hand, along with sleep problems. It is actually important for getting any kind of concerns regarding health to be addressed both for addressing any kind of worries in your life and also for dealing with any kind of physical health problem.

- **Attitude:** The easiest way of sleeping is when you feel relaxed and let go of all your concerns in life. Every one of us has had that one night when we just lie down all awake and worry about various things. Right before the time when you try to go to your bed, try to wind down everything. Try to be as less stimulated as possible and try to relax.

  It might actually be a bit tough in attaining all these because of the fast moving loves of today, but there are various relaxation techniques like taking a warm bath right before you sleep or practicing mindfulness can really help. In case you are not feeling sleepy, it is better to get up from the bed and try to do something which you love and get back to bed as you feel sleepy. Forcing yourself to sleep is not going to help you at all. You might opt for watching TV or scrolling down your social media, but doing so might cut off your sleep for the night, and you will end up having an unpleasant sleep. You can make a cup of warm milk for yourself if you find it difficult to fall sleep.

- **Environment:** The place where you sleep is of utter importance. The bed, along with your bedroom needs to be those places with which you can actually associate yourself while sleeping. In particular, playing games, watching TV or eating in your bed can also affect your sleep quality. Various factors play in determining sleep quality, such as level of noise, light, and temperature. In case you are still facing problem in falling asleep, you can opt for maintaining a sleep diary in which you can easily find your pattern of sleeping, and it can also help in identifying the actual problem.

- **Lifestyle:** The kind of life that you lead every day has a lot to do with your sleep quality. What you drink and what you eat can affect your sleep. Various kinds of stimulants, such as caffeine, can actually make it harder for you to sleep if you are a heavy coffee drinker. Having sugary or heavy meals right before going to bed might also make your sleep uncomfortable. You will say that alcohol helps in getting you to sleep and it is true, but it will play with the sleep quality at a later stage.

If you want to have a good night's sleep, try to exercise every day. But, note that exercising helps in releasing adrenaline, so if you opt for exercising in the evening time, it might be hard for you to sleep. Try to maintain a healthy lifestyle, which includes no form of addiction such as smoking or drinking, no watching TV for late hours, exercising every morning, and, if possible to try to opt for yoga to be precise. Yoga comes with the power of soothing our senses and calms down our mind and thus helps us in relaxing all our senses.

## How to kick away negative thoughts at the time of sleeping?

You need to understand that it is not only in your mind. When you have the habit of thinking about stressful and negative things right before going to bed can really keep you up all night. There are actually only a handful of people who might not have experienced this ever in their life. You are going to have a stressful day, a lot of work to be done tomorrow, or even the most random kind of reflections about any kind of past events that you cannot kick away before going to bed. You might even actually lose several hours of the day consistently to all your negative thoughts, which actually persist in real. It is properly established in the psychology that overthinking some unpleasant kinds of thoughts or even past events, is actually a risk factor for reduced sleep quality along with various disorders of human mood such as depression.

However, there are various ways in which you can easily kick away all your negative thoughts right before going to bed to have a good night's sleep. Let's have a look at some of them.

- **Heading for the bed earlier:** It has been found from various studies that people who tend to go to bed late have higher chances of having negative thoughts at the time of sleeping, which will ultimately lead to bad quality or even no sleep. The same thing also applies to all those people who sleep for a shorter period of time. Normal human beings need at least 7 hours of sleep every day to lead a healthy lifestyle. When you fail to sleep properly or go to bed late, it will actually be hampering your very own health.

  Try to move your time to bed up by 10-15 minutes every day for creating a perfect schedule, which will be allowing you to get enough amount of sleep at night. You can try out a consistent form of an early bedtime for noting down your sleep quality. When you go to bed early, you can give your body and mind more time to relax, and it will ultimately help in giving you a good night's sleep. Just do not force yourself to sleep and to relax as much as you can without any kind of worries or tension.

- **Talking with your inner-self in a positive way:** Another method which can be used for countering all the negative kind of thoughts is by practicing self-conversation which is very common with the therapists of a cognitive form of behavior. Self-talking does not mean negative self-talk, which generally involves the habits of focusing only on the cons of any particular situation and giving no importance to the pros, personalizing all blame, anticipating all the worst situations, and also polarizing in between bad and good with no in the middle. Self-talking needs to be practiced for bringing out all your worries which are of a positive nature.

The main idea behind this is that whenever you find yourself dwelling with the negative thoughts only in your mind, you try to assess its actual validity consciously and try to move on from there. In place of just holding on to or obsessing over all such things which went wrong in the past, try to look out for the solutions to all your life problems. Try doing something in order to refocus your entire attention. You can boost up your mood by thinking about those things which you are really grateful for.

- **Using a guided form of visualization or relaxation: a** Guided form of relaxation might turn out to be helpful in clearing up your mind and for taking off all your focus from the negative kind of thoughts. You can also opt for a therapist if you cannot do the same by yourself. If you are thinking about doing it on your own, there are various programs for guided relaxation. The traditional and ancient way of practicing guided relaxation will work by relaxing the body and followed by focusing on the way of breathing. Guided visualization requires you to visualize an image or scene in your mind for the sole purpose of grabbing all your attention.

  You can do this by thinking about something which you love, or you want in your life. You can also visualize the image of your lover which can help you in relaxing your mind and kicking out all the negative thoughts. Right before you start with this, try to calm yourself down and, if possible, try to be alone in the room. It will help in connecting your inner-self with your mind, and you will find it a lot more easy to get a good night's sleep.

- **Breathing with purpose:** When you breathe technically, you can easily promote the relaxation of your mind and can also reduce stress. It is somewhat similar to the technique of guided relaxation. The main idea behind this is to follow a fixed pattern of breathing, which will focus on some places of your physical body and will help in deleting all those thoughts which are actually bothering you and your daily sleep patterns. Effective breathing also helps in affecting the heart rate which also plays a deep part in making you feel relaxed and calm. The various techniques of breathing are:

1.  **Diaphragmatic breathing:** It is the technique of breathing deeply right through the stomach, followed by exhaling the air slowly.

2.  **Equal breathing:** This is the technique of breathing in which you inhale and exhale for exactly the same time frame at the count of 4-5 seconds continuously.

3.  **Resistance breathing:** It is the technique of breathing consistently in and out with your lips pursed and via your nose.

4.  **Breath moving:** This is the technique of breathing in which you assume that when you are inhaling, you are actually moving in the air right to your brain, and as you exhale, you are moving the air to the base of the spine.

- **Relaxing to music:** Music comes with the incredible power of soothing all your senses. It is often regarded as a powerful mode of therapy, as well. It helps in clearing all forms of stress as you listen to soft music, and it can also help in improving your focus along with concentration for clearing out all the negative thoughts from your mind. It has also been found that as music helps in dealing with stress, it can also be used for treating sleep disorders.

You can opt for music therapy by seeking help from the professional therapists who can guide you through various sessions and will help you in relaxing your mind and body. If you want, you can practice the same on your own by listening to soft music at low volume right before going to sleep. Try to close your eyes as you indulge yourself in this activity and give your best for throwing away all the worries and thoughts in your mind. Try to get the music inside your head, and you will find that you are able to sleep for much more time.

When you try to do it alone, try out some calming music without any kind of lyrics like nature tracks, soft instrumentals, or even classical music. Try to put on the songs and focus only on the sound along with the rhythm and breathing calmly. If you want, you can also hum with the pattern of music and lose yourself in it for changing the mindset. You can even change your sleeping schedule along with sleeping patterns as you indulge yourself in the act of music therapy for kicking away all the negative thoughts.

- **Having positive thoughts:** When you try to go to bed with negative thoughts in your mind, you might find it difficult to go to sleep. And even if you sleep, you are most likely to wake up in the middle of the night and start worrying about vague things. You can deal with this by trying to instill positive thoughts in your mind. This cannot be achieved readily, and you are required to practice the same regularly. Try to focus on the present and do not even think about the past. You will not be thinking about your future as well and just concentrate on the current situation. Try assuming yourself as the luckiest person on earth, and you will find yourself to be more motivated and relaxed. Negative thoughts generally come with the traits of unnecessary worrying which can be easily removed by thinking about the present situation and being positive.

When you have the habit of ruminating or overthinking all the negative forms of things, it might not be an easy task to kick them off. You are required to be consistent enough with all of these techniques as you try to remove all sorts of negative thoughts from your mind and concentrate on sleeping.

# Conclusion

As you are done with each and every teaching of this eBook, you are now capable of dealing with all the traits of overthinking. You are now empowered enough to create a clear picture of overthinking and all its effects on your life. This eBook must have also helped you to gain an apt idea about your inner-self and what all can be done for surviving from the negative effects of overthinking. You are your own boss, and you are the only one who can direct your mind in doing what is right.

With the help of this eBook, you must have also learned about various other aspects of human psychology, such as mindfulness, coping up with negativity and various others. You can easily learn the very ways of freeing yourself up from the grip of rumination by teaching your mind about what is right and what is wrong. When you overthink, you are most likely to ruin your entire life. You need to think about your own good. Overthinking comes with the power of making a small situation look like a monster, and it will, in turn, make you feel stressed.

So, if you are thinking about improving your mind, then start right away with the help of this eBook with a proper idea about dealing with overthinking. Remember, you are the one who can actually make or break your own future.

If you find this book helpful for yourself in any way, kindly leave a review on Amazon.

9 781671 673212